Animal Migrations

LEVEL 9

Teaching Tips

Gold Level 9

This book focuses on developing reading independence, fluency, and comprehension.

Before Reading

- Ask readers what they think the book will be about based on the title. Have them support their answer.

Read the Book

- Encourage readers to read silently on their own.
- As readers encounter unfamiliar words, ask them to look for context clues to see if they can figure out what the words mean. Encourage them to locate boldfaced words in the glossary and ask questions to clarify the meaning of new vocabulary.
- Allow readers time to absorb the text and think about each chapter.
- Ask readers to write down any questions they have about the book's content.

After Reading

- Ask readers to summarize the book.
- Encourage them to point out anything they did not understand and ask questions.
- Ask readers to review the questions on page 23. Have them go back through the book to find answers. Have them write their answers on a separate sheet of paper.

© 2024 Booklife Publishing
This edition is published by arrangement with Booklife Publishing.

North American adaptations © 2024 Jump!
5357 Penn Avenue South
Minneapolis, MN 55419
www.jumplibrary.com

Decodables by Jump! are published by Jump! Library.
All rights reserved. No part of this book may be reproduced in any form without written permission from the publisher.

Library of Congress Cataloging-in-Publication Data is available at www.loc.gov or upon request from the publisher.

ISBN: 979-8-88996-906-8 (hardcover)
ISBN: 979-8-88996-907-5 (paperback)
ISBN: 979-8-88996-908-2 (ebook)

Photo Credits
Images are courtesy of Shutterstock.com. With thanks to Getty Images, Thinkstock Photo and iStockphoto. Cover – rck_953. p4–5 – kavram, Nataliia Melnychuk. p6–7 – Nataliia Melnychuk, Nagel Photography. p8–9 – Sergey Uryadnikov, FotoRequest. p10–11 – Menno Schaefer, Dennis Stogsdill. p12–13 – liveostockimages, COULANGES. p14–15 – JHVEPhoto, Andrew Astbury. p16–17 – Brian E Kushner, showcake. p18–19 – Ondrej Prosicky, Zi Magine. p20–21 – Dudarev Mikhail, shmatkov.

Table of Contents

What Is a Habitat?

A **habitat** is the place where an animal or plant lives. A good habitat gives an animal everything it needs to live, such as food, water, and shelter. There are many types of habitats, and each one is different.

All animals need different things to survive, so animals live in habitats that meet their needs. Some animals have **adapted** to live in certain habitats. Animals that live in cold habitats might have thick fur to keep them warm.

What Does Migration Mean?

Migration is the movement of animals from one place to another. Some animals move short distances when they migrate, while others travel hundreds of miles. Some animals migrate from one type of habitat to another.

Migrating flock of snow geese

There are many reasons animals migrate. Animals often migrate to find better living conditions. This can be because of changing weather conditions or for food. Some animals, such as emperor penguins, migrate to find a **mate** and have young.

Arctic Terns

The Arctic tern has one of the longest migrations in the world. These birds travel from the Arctic to Antarctica and back again. This means they travel around 20,000 miles every year.

Arctic tern

Caribou

During summer, caribou live in grasslands. In winter, they travel south to find more food. Caribou have the longest land migration of any animal. They migrate in huge **herds** of up to 260,000 caribou.

The Great Migration

The Great Migration happens once a year in Africa. This migration includes more than one million wildebeest and many other animals, such as zebras. These animals migrate across Tanzania and Kenya to give birth and find food and water.

Wildebeest herd

Salmon

Most types of salmon are born in freshwater lakes. They migrate from the lakes to the sea to find food. After eating, salmon migrate back to the lakes to mate. Salmon migrate in groups called shoals.

Emperor Penguins

Emperor penguins live in Antarctica. Every year, penguins walk many miles across the ice to meet their mates. When the weather gets warmer and the ice starts to melt, they jump into the sea and swim away.

The Sardine Run

The sardine run is a migration of sardines that happens in South Africa. Millions of sardines migrate each year. Scientists are not sure why sardines migrate. During their migration, many sardines get eaten by hungry birds, sharks, and other animals.

Monarch Butterflies

Monarch butterflies migrate up to 3,000 miles. When it gets cold, monarch butterflies in the United States and Canada either travel to Mexico or California, where it is much warmer. Then they mate and lay their eggs.

Monarch butterflies

Arctic Foxes

Arctic foxes migrate to find **prey**. They eat small animals that can be hard to find on the ice. Sometimes, Arctic foxes follow polar bears across the ice so they can eat their leftovers without having to hunt.

Semipalmated Sandpipers

Semipalmated sandpipers are small birds that migrate during fall and spring each year. Before their journey, semipalmated sandpipers eat lots of food to give them plenty of energy. They fly all the way over the Atlantic Ocean without stopping!

Earthworms

Earthworms live in soil. Unlike most animals, they migrate vertically. Rather than traveling across the land, they migrate upward and downward. When it is cold, they bury themselves deeper in the soil to move away from the cold.

Earthworms

Whales

Many whale **species** migrate every year. They often find food in cold water but give birth in warmer water. Humpback whales have one of the longest migrations of any **mammal**. Some swim 5,000 miles.

Humpback whale

Polar Bears

Polar bears spend part of the year on sea ice. In the warmer months, the ice melts and the polar bears migrate to spend summer on land. When it is cold enough, the polar bears migrate back to the ice.

How Is Climate Change Affecting Migration?

Earth is getting hotter. This is **climate change**. Climate change is causing weather patterns to change. Animals rely on weather patterns to know when to migrate. These changes might make animals migrate at the wrong times.

Climate change is particularly bad for animals that live on ice. As Earth gets warmer, the sea ice melts faster. This means polar bears have to stay on land longer, where it is harder for them to find food.

Index

How to Use an Index

An index helps us find information in a book. Each word has a set of page numbers. These page numbers are where you can find information about that word.

Page numbers

Example: balloons 5, 8–10, 19

Important word

This means page 8, page 10, and all the pages in between. Here, it means pages 8, 9, and 10.

Questions

1. Which animal has the longest land migration?

2. How do Arctic foxes sometimes get food without hunting?

3. Why is climate change a problem for polar bears?

4. Using the Table of Contents, can you find which page you can read about the Great Migration?

5. Using the Index, can you find a page in the book about humpback whales?

6. Using the Glossary, can you define what climate change is?

Glossary

adapted:
Changed to suit different conditions.

climate change:
Changes in Earth's weather and climate over time.

habitat:
The place where an animal or plant is usually found.

herds:
Large groups of animals that live and move together.

mammal:
A warm-blooded animal that usually has hair or fur and usually gives birth to live babies. A female mammal produces milk to feed her young.

mate:
The male or female partner of a pair of animals that come together to produce young.

migration:
The movement of animals from one place to another.

prey:
Animals that are hunted by other animals for food.

species:
One of the groups into which similar animals and plants are divided.